String of Miracles
poems of love

MINDA MAGERO

STRING OF MIRACLES
Poems of Love

An Aenzzi Book

Published by Aenzzi Press

Los Angeles, California

Copyright © 2016 Minda Magero

All rights reserved.

Cover artwork by Minda Magero

Cover design by Kanyi Muraguri

ISBN-13: 978-0997420104
ISBN-10: 0997420103

DEDICATION

To all who are constantly learning to love;
constantly *choosing* to love.

OTHER TITLES BY THE AUTHOR

The Book of Mysteries (2008, Novum Press)

CONTENTS

Acknowledgments	i
SPRING	1
Unspoken Thoughts	2
First Move	3
Don't Hide Your Face	4
Chance	5
Chemistry	6
Heartstrings	7
Savory Moments	8
Treasured	9
Fiery Love	10
SUMMER	13
Love Is	14
The List	15
Dreams Come True	16
My Love is not Lazy	17
Choosing Love	18
The Gentleman	19
Haven	20

AUTUMN	23
Windy Blue Romance	24
When I am Gone	25
Present	26
Better Together	27
Return	28
Wasted	29
No Gift	30
WINTER	33
Snuffed Out	34
Hurt	35
Fruitless	36
Night Letters	37
INDIAN SUMMER	39
String of Miracles	40
Celebrated	41
Reborn	42
Love Letter—25th Anniversary	43

ACKNOWLEDGMENTS

Over a 6-year period, I interviewed many, many people—friends, acquaintances, strangers—about their experiences in love. I am greatly indebted to them for sharing their experiences in and insights on love. My poems are so much richer for those stories.
In addition, *Love Is* was a collaborative work that arose from different people's responses to that phrase when I posted it on social media in 2010. To all of you, whose generosity has contributed to this work, thank you.

spring

Love is
waking moment
excitement, rifling
through yesterday's
memories
stumbling upon
today's
joyous anticipation.

Unspoken Thoughts

I long to say so many things
like I'm so grateful that you
take time to be with me.
But words are never there
when they should be
and so much stands between us
still unsaid.
Smoky thoughts.
Drifting fragments.
Will we ever speak of them?

First Move

whenever I catch you watching me
I am jolted to find I've been watching you
what is it about you that draws me in?
what fascination do I hold for you?
can you teach me the steps of this dance of romance?
it seems I stumble each time I try

will you be the one whose lead I can follow?
could this be the dance I've been waiting for?
maybe it is only a practice session
we cannot know until we try
so I think for now
the big question remains
who will first make the move
that puts us on the dance floor?

Don't Hide Your Face

Turn towards me and meet my gaze
with messages words cannot express.
Do stay awhile, don't shy away
let me drink from the pools in your eyes.
Stand close, your scent embracing me
deep rumblings of your chest unsettling me.
Touch me, by chance, delightful tremors
leave in the wake of skin contact.

Chance

Where this road leads
I have never ventured
now fascinating, now formidable.
Shall I take a chance
fan this unexpected flame
tend this one-of-a-kind fire
burning here?
Explore this unknown quantity
open surprising doors
maybe even find treasure
in unlikely places?
Will we prove to be made of
dust and ashes
blown away
by the breath
of slightest wind?
Or dare we hope we are made of
sterner stuff
to survive hurricanes
to dance together again
and again?

Chemistry

They speak of Cupid's arrow
from whose tip the spark of *eros*
flies to inflame two strangers.

But they forget to mention that
every untended fire finally dies
and *eros* alone makes no lasting flame.

Eros is merely the white, hot center
sometimes with blues supporting it
or yellows and oranges of steadiness.

Ludus, that playful spice of mystery
must join in to keep him burning.
Stack *philia* onto that flaming pile
the joys of knowing and being known.
And what of *pragma* for the long haul?
They together sustain that beautiful blaze.

Heartstrings

Jungle cat glides across crowded room
laser-sharp gaze drawing my head up
Who are you, what
have you done to me?
When did I become so
aware of you?
Why is it
my body sings when
you are near?
Where learned you to pluck
the strings of my heart?
How is it my blood
dances to your tune?

Savory Moments

I savor these delectable moments with you
luxuriate in discourse
that fattens my soul
delight in your wonderful hugs and
our laughter.

Sitting close to you here on this couch
I drink in the beauty of your form
There you sit singing
beautiful love melodies
here my heart sways at your song.

My head blissfully rests on your heart
strong arms encircle and hold me tight
magical stillness
beautiful whispers of love
You hold my gaze again
thrills course through my frame
and I savor this moment
I dream.

Treasured

(for the tiger, gratefully)
Where memories made
on walks with others
always faded at daybreak
like old photographs
our first walk ages well
like a cask of fine wine
richer and more delightful
with the passage of time.

I blossomed for you
beneath starry skies
like Night Blooming Jasmine
and Casablanca Lilies.
Your adoration
unlocked
my fragrance.

Fiery Love

Some days when I walk into your space
you're smoldering like embers
I'm kindling for the fire.
The winds pick up
sparks crackle between us
the temperature inches towards boiling point.

But because I love you
and you honor me
we choose not to light this fire today.
We choose to rein in our passions
until we seal our covenant.
For a fire contained
will warm us and our children
but a fire that rages
will raze our house to the ground.

STRING OF MIRACLES

MINDA MAGERO

summer

Love—a mature
bergamot tree
lush green leaves
heavy ripe fruit
rewarding
endurance.

Love is

Love is a rare exotic orchid
budding, blossoming, growing
More beautiful with each dawn.
A rainy Sunday morning
a brilliant sunset
a comforting fire on a chilly winter's night.

It is my very own magic carpet ride
unwavering acceptance
a soft place to fall.
Encouragement, affection
the freedom to be real
the sweetest, most intoxicating breath of life.

Love makes the choice to engage, stay aware
expressing it in that secret smile
the special glint in your eye.
It lavishes tender, soothing embraces
in life's chaotic ambushes.
Love always will be the greatest thing.

The List

He's not quite the one she sought
still he comes as a nice surprise
all the basic qualities intact
she should know because she's checked.
Open heart and gracious speech
valuing her and loving life

His particular brand of handsome
greatly differs from her dreams
sandy hair, blue eyes, Viking features
are the things she had in mind.
What he brings though is dark hair
shimmering like a raven's coat
skin that's olive, eyes so brown
he reminds her of a desert prince.

By his heart she's captivated
rendered breathless by his gaze
He is just the one she dreamed of
and she's laughing at her list.

Dreams Come True
for Jana & Matt

I dreamed of the day you would enter my life
and hoped you would look past my failings and flaws
I dreamed a dream so beautiful
half of it fulfilled would have sufficed.
But when my path and yours crossed
I found you surpassed my grandest thoughts.

Your tender words and gentle ways
unveil new wonders within me
just as the lightly-fingered rains
of spring coax flowers from the trees.
Your love—fresh as the morning dew—
brings all my fears to nothingness.

This day births our dream of shared bliss
of adventures and happiness and thrills
a dream of a lifetime of togetherness
whether it rains, or whether it shines.
With the words *I do* we seal the vow
To dream new dreams that will come true.

My Love is Not Lazy

When I chose to call you my love
I became a student of your ways
showing interest in your thoughts
in the way they shape your life.
Tokyo is on your bucket list
as are Prague and Zanzibar
A 400-page novel in a hammock
is your favorite way to relax.
Buttermilk pancakes with strawberries
put a smile on your Saturday-morning face
sometimes you want potatoes with your steak
other times you prefer broccoli.
Middle-squeezed toothpaste tubes
dirty laundry lying all over
are sure ways you make you mad.
Wednesdays are for date nights and cuddling
handwritten notes are home runs.
My love is not lazy
I won't let it rust
I keep learning how to love you.

Choosing Love

We were young in love
walking hand in hand
the sky seemed bluer, the grass so much greener
as though love had painted
new colors in old places.
I loved you then.

I loved you then when choosing love was easy
when a look was all it took
to capture my heart
and send it on wings to the tops of the clouds.

I love you now
I choose you daily even when
our morning breath and bed heads
hold no sex appeal
I honor you always above
all others who may catch my eye.
I love you now.

Love has changed from constant headiness
to the more sedate pace of intentionality
I gift you with my friendship
with caring actions meaningful to you
it costs me more now
but
I love you more.

The Gentleman

Consistency
this marks the gentleman
opening doors, not once
but every time
Kindhearted
he puts your needs before his
is gracious, noble
levelheaded, respectful.
Chivalrous
he walks you to your door
makes sure you're safe
before he drives away.
Gentle
he shields you with his strength
yet tender enough
to share in your grief.
Gallant and patient
he keeps the peace
even when sometimes
he must confront.
Generous, considerate
honorable, faithful
savoir-faire is his middle name.

Haven

Your voice is a gentle, soothing stream
flowing out like lazy ocean waves
deliciously lapping at feet.

Your voice is the sound of comfort
in a world filled with noisy, strident calls
its cadence marked with infectious joy.

What a precious gift is your voice!
what a treasure are conversations
your speaking building a haven.

STRING OF MIRACLES

MINDA MAGERO

autumn

Love is heartache
when
storms thunder in
darkening brilliant
skies.

Windy Blue Romance

    Out of the blue, love. He speaks love. Speaking he speaks from the blue love. Pursues blue pursuing blue speaking the blue love pursues. Attracted. Yes she says yes yes. Falling falling falls falling in love she falls. Fallen.
    Wild wind the romance here there planning, wildly windy wild romance plans, happy happy happy wild plans fighting. Happy fighting fight fight. Sour.
    No he says no never loved you. Incredulous. Cracks cracking shattering heart shattering cracking shattering
        heart shards everywhere.

When I Am Gone

Do not by unsaid, not-done things
drive me away from you.
do not erase me carelessly
from the pages of your life.

You will miss me when I am gone.

The little, pretty notes I wrote
to give encouragement
the peaceful sense of presence
I bring into a room
Who will give ear to your
thoughts as I did
know you are present before
glimpsing you?
The sweet thrill
that you knew with me
could you find it with another?

You will miss me when I am gone
though now you pretend not to care.

Present

Don't let me forget your face

the sound of your voice
the touch of your hands
the scent of your skin
the taste of your lips.

Don't leave me to fight
my battles alone
Don't dance with me
from afar.
If you take my hand
I will journey with you.

Better Together

How many times have we
walked away
only to turn back seeking
familiar embraces
comfortable togetherness
stimulating talks
electrifying touches.
Why can't we stay
together?

Return

I'm willing you to think
of me
tonight.
To miss me as
I do you, to
remember
our chemistry.

I'm willing you to
dwell on
how good we were together
for each other
each with the other.

Remember, my love.
Return.

Wasted

you will never give me what i want
you do not know how to love me

you wasted all the chances given you
i have no more hours left for you

No Gift

He's kissed more lips
than he dares admit
held hands with dozens
whose names he forgot
dipped his stick in each
open honey-pot
nothing special saved to
gift the one he loves.

STRING OF MIRACLES

MINDA MAGERO

winter

Love is a
hard-to-find splinter
lodged
beneath skin
festering
till
pulled out.

Snuffed Out

you chose and
gasp
I wasn't the one.
the flame in me died. It
may never reignite.

Hurt

lips sealed
eyes veiled
heart stowed
poker face
all ears

Fruitless

What use is love
when
you feel differently?
'Tis better then
never
to have loved at all.

Night Letters

These letters I write night after night
you will never read them
I will never send them.
I write to think, to understand
to unravel the threads of yesteryears.
Threads of our play
threads of our fights
of laughter, tears
mundane in-betweens.
When did I stop choosing you?
Was it the coffee-slurping
the open-mouthed chewing?
Or was it all those times I forgot to replace
the used-up toilet paper roll?
These letters by night
questions you'll never see
why did you stop choosing to love me?

indian summer

Love: unexpected
sweetness
second chances
delights waiting
in the wings.

String of Miracles

They'd always imagined love to be simple.
Easy, even.
Two people met and fell in love
the rest was history.
But time and life have questioned
dismantled and questioned again
things once taken for granted.
Love has hardly been simple
nor easy.

She missed all the clues
when his heart was hers
he had just moved on
when she finally knew.

Detours, regrets
mixed signals, years later
paths leading together again.
Heart talks, apologies
tears hugs kisses
Love survived
through
A string of miracles.

Celebrated

I had never known so much kindness
until he came along.
A match made in heaven
fell into my lap
at the ripe age of 49.

In his eyes I'm a jewel
he designs my clothes
calls me his work of art
plays piano when I sing
doesn't mind my loud voice
offers me his silent strength.

I have never been so celebrated
he is better than all my hopes.

Reborn

There are no good men left
this her lament
thoroughly unwilling to
make the same mistake twice.
She's not my type, he'd insisted
burned once, he also twice shy.
That inside voice counseled him:
you don't know what's good for you.

Paths bend towards each other
nearness reveals treasures not seen
from a distance
laments and complaints dissipate
beautiful shoots of tenderness appear.
Love is born.
Again.

Love Letter—25th Anniversary

My darling, we've made it this far! Looking back on 25 years of loving you, I can't imagine having journeyed with anyone else.

Exhilarating attraction brought us together at first, then we built a solid friendship that carries us through. A foundation from which we
negotiate hardships
disagreements
glaring differences between us
with a deep regard for one another.

I know no one else as well as I do you, no one knows me better than you—even with worlds still left to discover as we each continually develop and change.

I loved the person you were when we met, and greatly enjoy whom you've grown into. I treasure who we are together, and would never trade it for fortune or fame. You're the lover I share all sweet intimacies with, the companion with me on unexciting days. You're the thought that puts a smile on my face, even though sometimes you make me insane. You're the partner I
travel the world with
seize the day with
eat dinner with
share hopes and dreams with.

I've so many memories of you holding my hand
in laughter and joy
in pain and distress.
You're a safe place for my soul.
This thing of wonder we've built together, let's make it last for the rest of our lives.

STRING OF MIRACLES

ABOUT THE AUTHOR

Minda Magero is a lover of words—reading them, writing them, dreaming about them. Her first collection of poetry *The Book of Mysteries* (Novum Press LLC, USA) was published in 2008. Her poetry has also been published in the literary journal *Kwani?* (Kwani Trust, 2012) and in the soon-coming anthology *Multiverse: Kenyan Poetry in English Since 2003* (Kwani Trust, 2016).
Her prose includes the essay *Memoirs: My Primary School Experience in Africa* published in the textbook *Cambridge Checkpoint English Book 3* (Hodder Education, 2011-2015), widely used in schools around the world. Her articles have been published at *AfricaOnTheBlog.com* and *KenyaImagine.com*.

In addition to writing, Minda pursues other creative outlets, including performance, painting and music. She experiments at mindamagero.com.

www.ingramcontent.com/pod-product-compliance
Lightning Source LLC
Chambersburg PA
CBHW070543080426
42453CB00029B/1017